VOLUNTEERING FOR THE
HOMELESS

by Walt K. Moon

BrightPoint Press

San Diego, CA

BrightPoint Press

© 2022 BrightPoint Press
an imprint of ReferencePoint Press, Inc.
Printed in the United States

For more information, contact:
BrightPoint Press
PO Box 27779
San Diego, CA 92198
www.BrightPointPress.com

LIBRARY OF CONGRESS CATALOGING-IN-PUBLICATION DATA

Names: Moon, Walt K., author.
Title: Volunteering for the homeless / by Walt K. Moon.
Description: San Diego, CA : BrightPoint Press, 2022. | Series: Get involved | Includes
    bibliographical references and index. | Audience: Grades 7-9
Identifiers: LCCN 2021009629 (print) | LCCN 2021009630 (eBook) | ISBN 9781678201340
    (hardcover) | ISBN 9781678201357 (eBook)
Subjects: LCSH: Voluntarism--Juvenile literature. | Homeless persons--Services for--Juvenile
    literature.
Classification: LCC HN49.V64 M66 2022 (print) | LCC HN49.V64 (eBook) | DDC 302/.14--
    dc23
LC record available at https://lccn.loc.gov/2021009629
LC eBook record available at https://lccn.loc.gov/2021009630

CONTENTS

AT A GLANCE

- Homelessness is a major issue in the United States today.

- People become homeless for many reasons. They may not have money for housing. They may lose their jobs suddenly. Medical issues and legal trouble may be factors too.

- A homeless shelter gives people experiencing homelessness a safe place to stay. Volunteers can help check people in. They can supervise kids, serve meals, keep the shelter clean, and do other tasks.

- Soup kitchens are places that serve free, fresh food. Volunteers can serve food, greet guests, wash dishes, clean tables, and do other tasks. They can also help connect people experiencing homelessness with resources that can help them further.

- Point-in-time counts are counts of the number of people experiencing homelessness in an area. These counts affect government funding for homelessness programs. Volunteers can go into communities. They perform the counts. They interview people experiencing homelessness. They collect important data.

- Donation drives are organized events in which people collect donations for particular causes, including homelessness. Volunteers can run or participate in these drives.

MAKING A DIFFERENCE

For Carlos, volunteering at the homeless shelter was personal. It wasn't long ago that his uncle had experienced homelessness. Uncle Gabriel had worked hard for many years. Then he got sick. He lost his job. His medical bills added up. Suddenly he couldn't pay his rent.

Homeless shelters provide beds for people experiencing homelessness.

Uncle Gabriel spent time at a homeless shelter. The people there gave him food and a place to shower. He could wash his clothes and **socialize** with people. He got help finding a new job and a place to live. Within a few months, Uncle Gabriel was able to get stable housing. The shelter had been a big help. Now Carlos wanted to help other people in the same way.

Carlos had just turned sixteen, so he could volunteer on his own. He headed in through the glass front doors. He greeted the front desk workers. They were volunteers too. Sometimes Carlos helped out at the desk. Other times he served dinner. Today he would be cleaning up the shelter. It wasn't the most exciting work.

Homeless shelters need people to help keep the facilities clean.

But it was important to make the shelter a

welcoming place.

He grabbed a mop and cleaned the

tile floors in the hallway. He passed by the

rooms where people got help with health problems or were trained for new job skills. Nearby were the rooms where volunteers helped young kids with homework. Carlos smiled warmly as a resident walked past him in the hall. Next he vacuumed the carpets. Then he got a rag and spray bottle and washed the windows.

When Carlos finished, he took a moment to admire his work. The shelter looked great. Cleaning made it look like a safe, inviting place. It felt good to make a difference.

People become homeless for a number of different reasons.

HOMELESSNESS TODAY

Homelessness is a major issue in the United States today. In 2019, the **federal** government did a count. It found that approximately 570,000 Americans were homeless. That's about as many people as are in the entire state of Wyoming.

Collecting donations is an important way volunteers can help.

There are many reasons people become homeless. They may be unable to afford housing. They may lose their jobs suddenly.

Substance use disorders or other mental illnesses can worsen these issues. Medical problems and legal trouble can also contribute.

Volunteers can help out at homeless shelters or soup kitchens. They can help count the homeless population in their area. This affects the amount of government funding available to address homelessness in the community. Volunteers can also set up donation drives. These events collect the supplies that people experiencing homelessness need the most. All of these types of volunteering can make a difference.

CHAPTER ONE

HOW CAN I VOLUNTEER AT A HOMELESS SHELTER?

There are many different types of shelters for people experiencing homelessness. In general, shelters give people a safe place to stay. People are protected from harsh weather.

Homeless shelters may help people with mental health issues.

They stay in shelters while they search for

permanent housing.

Shelters also provide services. People

can get help with mental or physical health

issues. They can get help finding jobs or housing. People can receive job training. Such services can help address the reasons people become homeless.

Homeless shelters usually have a large number of beds in a shared open area. There may be spaces for eating meals. A shelter may have showers and laundry machines. There may be rooms where adults can get job assistance and kids can get homework help.

Some shelters are open only at night. They are meant to give people a safe place to sleep. Other shelters give people a place

A shelter may have tutors who help kids with school assignments.

to stay during the day. Homeless shelters

are usually meant for a stay of a few months

or less. **Transitional** housing is another

type of shelter. These places may have

Front desk volunteers welcome people to the shelter.

individual or shared apartments. People can

access more services to help them prepare

to move out. They may stay in transitional

housing for a few years.

Volunteers play important roles in many

homeless shelters. They help the staff keep

the shelter running smoothly. And they also learn more about homelessness itself. One volunteer at a shelter in Minnesota said, "Volunteering here has shown me another side to shelters. There are so many **misconceptions** about people who are experiencing homelessness. The people here are just like anyone else. They just ended up in a bad situation."[1]

WHAT CAN VOLUNTEERS DO?

Volunteers can help at shelters in many ways. A shelter might have a front desk at the entrance. Volunteers can greet people who arrive. They can check people in so the

Volunteers can help clean floors at a shelter.

shelter has a record of them. They can give

out information as people come in.

Volunteers can also help out with kids

at the shelter. They can help staff care

for infants and toddlers. They can read to

older kids and help them with homework. Volunteers can oversee group games or craft projects.

Providing meals is an important mission for shelters. Volunteers can help with this too. They can make coffee and serve food. They can also eat dinner with people in the shelter. Volunteers can explain the resources available at the shelter. Or they can simply socialize with the people there.

Keeping the shelter clean is another important job. Volunteers can sweep, mop, and vacuum floors. They can clean windows and do laundry.

Volunteers can also help out with fundraising. Shelters may get some money from the government, but they also rely on donations. Volunteers can write thank-you notes to people who donate to the shelter. They can address and mail fundraising letters. They can help set up fundraising

COVID-19 AND HOMELESS SHELTERS

The COVID-19 pandemic spread around the world in 2020. This created new challenges for homeless shelters. Staying a safe distance apart is hard in tightly packed shelters. Many volunteers dropped out. They did not want to risk catching or spreading COVID-19. Shelters searched for ways to keep running during this time.

Behind-the-scenes work can be just as rewarding as other types of volunteer work.

events. These tasks help ensure the shelter

can keep operating.

BENEFITS OF VOLUNTEERING

Volunteering at homeless shelters gives

people a chance to directly help those in

need. This work can make an important impact in the lives of people experiencing homelessness. Collin Gortner, a volunteer at a shelter in Indiana, explained, "Volunteering and trying to make my community a better place for everyone is really important to me, and the homeless is a population that I really care about and really enjoy serving."[2]

This type of service is also a good fit if people are interested in political issues around housing. They can see how homelessness affects their communities. They can get experience for future careers involved in this issue. Finally, it can be a great way to meet new people and broaden one's perspective.

GETTING INVOLVED

To get involved in homeless shelter volunteering, people should research local shelters. Each shelter works differently

KEY SKILLS

There are several key skills that are useful for volunteers at homeless shelters. Volunteers should have friendly and respectful attitudes. People coming to these shelters have a wide range of backgrounds. An environment of respect is important. Volunteers should also be reliable. The work that shelters do is crucial to their guests. By showing up on time, volunteers help keep shelters running smoothly.

and has different opportunities. The

requirements may vary too.

There are usually age requirements.

These may be different for different tasks.

For example, volunteers might need to

be sixteen to work at the front desk.

They might need to be eighteen to teach

self-defense classes for adults. They may

be able to help serve meals at age twelve

but need an adult with them until they are

age sixteen.

A potential volunteer must apply to the

shelter. Then a staff member interviews

her. There may be a **background check**.

Self-defense classes can help people experiencing homelessness stay safe.

If the person is accepted, there may be an orientation. The person may go through training. She might even follow a shelter worker for a day to learn how the shelter runs. Volunteers often need to commit to working for a certain amount of time.

CHAPTER TWO

HOW CAN I VOLUNTEER AT A SOUP KITCHEN?

A soup kitchen is a place that serves free, fresh food. Some people who use soup kitchens are homeless. Others may have places to live, but they cannot afford food. Soup kitchens ensure that all of these people have nutritious meals. This is important in staying healthy.

Volunteers may eat meals and chat with those being served at a soup kitchen.

Soup kitchens became popular in the 1930s during the Great Depression. This was a severe **economic** downturn. Companies failed. Many people lost their jobs. They struggled to pay for food.

Soup kitchens helped keep people fed. They served soup and bread. These foods are inexpensive and filling.

Soup kitchens are still widespread today. They serve more than just soup. But the original name continues to be used. They usually serve hot meals in a group dining area. Some also give away meals in bags for people to take with them. Soup kitchens might give clothing or **hygiene** products to their guests too.

Modern soup kitchens are often run by churches and charities. They usually rely on donations to operate. People can donate

Soup kitchen volunteers often serve food.

money so that the kitchen can purchase food. They may also donate food directly. People donate their time too. Many soup kitchens rely on volunteers.

WHAT CAN VOLUNTEERS DO?

The main volunteering job at soup kitchens is serving food. This is the heart of the soup

kitchen's mission. But there are other ways
to help too. Volunteers may greet guests
when they come to the kitchen. They can
help refill empty food containers. They
can wash dishes, and they can clean tables
after people finish their meals.

YEAR-ROUND HELP

Soup kitchens often have plenty of volunteers
during holidays such as Thanksgiving. But they
need to serve food all year long. Volunteers
should try to go at less popular times. They
can also commit to helping on a regular
basis. They can talk to the soup kitchen's
volunteer coordinator to find out what would be
most helpful.

Volunteers may also sit and talk with people eating meals. They can listen to what the guests have to say. Kitchens want the people who eat there to feel welcome. All of the kitchen's volunteers and staff can help with this goal.

Michael Ottley helps run a soup kitchen in New York. In an interview, he spoke about how important volunteers are. He said, "It's more than just feeding the hungry and the working poor, it's an opportunity to help a neighbor in need, whether that means you are plating their meal, connecting . . . them with social services or

Volunteers at soup kitchens may hand out groceries.

career prep resources, or providing them

with donated toiletries or clothing."[3]

BENEFITS OF VOLUNTEERING

Hot, nutritious meals can make a big

difference for people experiencing

homelessness. These meals can help people stay healthy. Coming in for meals gives people a reason to get out of harsh weather. People get a chance to talk with staff, volunteers, and fellow guests at the soup kitchen. These social connections can make people feel better. They can improve people's mental health. Volunteers help make all this possible. This can be a rewarding experience.

Nicholas volunteered at a New York City soup kitchen. He made sure the food line ran smoothly. He also filled up food containers as needed. He said, "Coming

Volunteers can connect with other people as they work.

here has opened up another part of my life.

It hit me in my heart directly. It's a pleasure

to see how people light up so easily just

with a simple meal."[4]

Volunteers can make connections of

their own through this work. They can get

to know their fellow workers at the soup kitchen. They can meet the guests who come in. The guests may have different backgrounds than the volunteers. Getting to know them can provide people with new perspectives on their communities.

GETTING INVOLVED

There are soup kitchens all over the country. The first step in volunteering is to find a local one. Nearby churches and local governments may help connect volunteers to soup kitchens. People can also search online for kitchens near them.

The next step is to talk to the volunteer coordinator at the soup kitchen. Different soup kitchens may have different age requirements. They may have different kinds of tasks for volunteers. They may have

SAFETY FIRST

When serving food, there are important safety rules volunteers should remember. They should tie back their hair, or they should wear a bandana or hairnet. That way hair won't fall into the food. Volunteers should remove jewelry that could fall off. They should wash their hands before starting a shift. They should also wash their hands after using the bathroom. Finally, volunteers should stay home if they feel sick. They do not want to risk spreading disease.

Some churches run soup kitchens.

It is important for soup kitchen volunteers to be welcoming.

different time commitments. The volunteer coordinator can provide all this information.

Volunteers at soup kitchens must be flexible. The kitchen may need help with many types of tasks. Volunteers should be ready to help however they can. They should also be kind to guests. It is important to make the soup kitchen a welcoming place. Finally, they should treat volunteering as a job. They should be on time. They should be reliable workers. They should be responsible.

CHAPTER THREE

HOW CAN I VOLUNTEER WITH POINT-IN-TIME COUNTS?

A point-in-time count is a count of the people experiencing homelessness in an area. It is done in the last week of January each year. The count includes both sheltered and unsheltered people.

Cities count the number of people experiencing homelessness so they know how many resources they need to help those people.

The goal is to collect accurate data about homelessness in that area.

The US Department of Housing and Urban Development (HUD) provides funding for homelessness programs. It requires communities to do these counts to get funding. Each year, communities must count sheltered people experiencing homelessness. They must count unsheltered people every two years. However, many communities do this count annually too.

WHO IS COUNTED?

During the point-in-time count, some communities may count people who are living with family or friends because they have lost their own housing. They may also count people living in medical facilities or jails. These people do not match the HUD definition of homeless. They are not included in that part of the count. Communities may collect this data for local homelessness programs.

HUD gathers data from around the country. It provides a report on homelessness to Congress each year. Together, all this data shows how the nation is doing in fighting homelessness. The data can also increase awareness of the issue. It can lead to more resources going toward ending homelessness.

In individual communities, point-in-time counts can help local groups fight homelessness. They can track how local efforts are doing. They can see which programs are working and which need improvement.

Unsheltered people include people sleeping on the streets and those living in their cars.

Local governments and organizations run the point-in-time counts. Paid staff may help lead the counts. But they usually rely on volunteer help. Volunteers go out into the community and do the counting.

WHAT CAN VOLUNTEERS DO?

Volunteers play an important role in counting unsheltered people. These people may be in a wide variety of places. They may be living on the streets or in abandoned buildings. They might be found in parks, alleys, parking lots, and many other places. The job of volunteers is to find these people and count them accurately.

Volunteers work in teams for safety. There are always other volunteers nearby. They approach people experiencing homelessness. Some people may be interested in talking. They may want to share their stories. Other people may not want to talk. It's important for volunteers to respect each person's wishes. Volunteers must be sure to treat people experiencing homelessness with **dignity**.

If people say they don't want to talk, volunteers thank them for their time and

GETTING PRACTICE

Some people have a tough time talking to strangers. It may be useful to practice beforehand. Volunteers can role-play with each other before doing the count. This can help them become more comfortable with the survey questions. They can practice asking questions and responding to people.

step away. Volunteers then fill out a survey form with any information possible. This might include the person's location, gender, and estimated age.

If a person does want to talk, volunteers can collect more information. They might ask for the person's name and birth date. This ensures that each person is counted only once. They might ask how the person became homeless. They might ask if the person is a military veteran. The exact questions may vary from community to community. The local group organizing the count may provide volunteers with a

Volunteers fill out information about the people they interview during a point-in-time count.

script. This can make it easier to gather

consistent data.

Volunteers fill out all this information

on a survey. When they are done, they

should thank the person for his or her

time. The organizing group may give the volunteers pamphlets or handouts about resources available to people experiencing homelessness. Volunteers can hand these to people they have counted. Finally, the volunteers return their surveys to their team leaders.

BENEFITS OF VOLUNTEERING

The point-in-time count is an important part of fighting homelessness. An accurate count helps the government direct resources to the right places. It helps communities understand what works and what doesn't. It helps the nation track how the fight against homelessness is going. Volunteers come away with the satisfaction of assisting this important mission.

Katie Vela helps run a point-in-time count in Texas. She explained how important it is: "This is really critical data for us. It's a good measurement to see, year over year, how we're doing with homelessness."[5]

On a personal level, volunteers can also learn more about homelessness in their communities. They have the chance to talk to people experiencing homelessness. They learn these people's stories. Gaining a better understanding of the community

POINT-IN-TIME COUNTS, 2010–2019

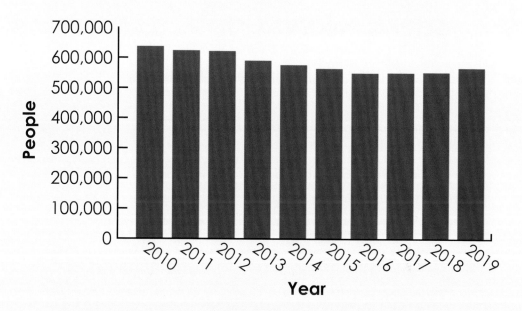

Source: "2019 Point in Time Estimates of Homelessness in the US: 2007–2019 Point-in-Time Estimates by State (XLSX)," US Department of Housing and Urban Development, 2019. www.hud.gov.

This graph shows the total number of people experiencing homelessness in the United States each year from 2010 to 2019. The data comes from individual point-in-time counts in each state. It was combined into a single report by HUD.

can be rewarding. It may inspire volunteers

to help address homelessness in other

ways too.

GETTING INVOLVED

To get started, a volunteer should contact the organization in his area that runs point-in-time counts. An online search can help him find it. The organization will have contact information for the people in charge of the count. A person can learn how the count works in his community. He can figure out what day it will be held. He can learn how to volunteer his time.

When a person is ready to volunteer, he should make sure he has the right gear. Point-in-time counts are held in January. The weather is often cold during this time of

People can often find information about local point-in-time counts online.

the year. A volunteer should have the right

clothing. He should also have comfortable

shoes. There is likely to be a lot of walking.

A backpack is useful too. It can hold

survey forms, snacks, water, and any other

supplies the volunteer needs.

It is important to dress for the weather during a point-in-time count.

For organizers, the safety of their volunteers is extremely important. They will share information about the best ways to stay safe. In general, it's important for volunteers to stay aware of their surroundings. They should always be with at least one other person. They should stick to places that are well lit, and they should use flashlights if needed. If they feel unsafe in a place, they should leave right away.

CHAPTER FOUR

HOW CAN I VOLUNTEER WITH A DONATION DRIVE?

A donation drive is an organized event to collect donations. These events can help out many kinds of causes. They can be useful for organizations fighting homelessness. Donation drives can bring in needed supplies and funding.

People drop off items such as clothes at donation drives.

This can make a big difference for people experiencing homelessness.

Donation drives collect many types of items. Some benefit young families. They may include diapers, formula, and baby wipes. Book drives may bring in books for children to read. Hygiene products are always needed. Soap, shampoo, toothpaste, and women's hygiene products make a big difference for people. In hot climates, sunscreen, water bottles, and sunglasses may be needed. In cold climates, people may need coats, gloves, and warm socks.

People can organize a donation drive in their area. This is a great way to multiply their efforts. They can get more people involved. They can collect many more donations than they could alone. People

Volunteers may need to help organize items received at a donation drive.

volunteer their time to help put these

drives together.

GETTING INVOLVED

The first step in setting up a donation

drive is asking for help. These drives can

be complicated events. There are many tasks to be done. There is a lot to manage. Someone needs to be in charge. Someone needs to spread the word and promote the event. People need to collect and store the donations that come in. People need to transport the donations to the place that is receiving them. One person could do a few of these tasks. But it is easier when working as a team. Family and friends may be willing to help out.

The next step is to talk to local organizations fighting homelessness. These places likely have experience with

Items from donation drives may be given to food shelves. Volunteers can help stock the shelves.

donation drives. They will know what kinds of supplies the community needs most. They may also have tips on running a successful drive.

In the weeks leading up to the drive, it is important to spread the word. People can send emails and make social media posts. They can put up flyers or send postcards. They can make announcements at school, work, or places of worship. People can talk to the local news media. They may want to do a story on the donation drive.

When spreading the word about a donation drive, people should include a few

Doing interviews with local radio stations can help raise awareness of the donation drive.

important things. It may be helpful to set a

clear goal. For example, the goal could be

to get a total of 500 clothing items. Having

a target like this may motivate people

to donate and reach the goal. It is also

important to have a specific list of what

is needed. For example, a flyer could list

socks, underwear, gloves, and coats as

desired items. People should explain where

and when donations will be accepted.

Finally, they should make it clear who is

SUPPLY KITS

Homeless shelters may have volunteers put together kits of donated supplies. Each kind of kit is for a different use. A shelter welcome kit is for people who are just arriving at the shelter. It might include a pillow, bedsheets, and a bath towel. A laundry kit is for those washing their clothes at the shelter. It might have detergent and dryer sheets in it.

running the drive and where donations are going to.

Once donations start coming in, people can take pictures of the growing piles of items. They can take photos when delivering the donations too. Then they can post the pictures on social media. This can help spread awareness of the drive and of the need for donations in general. It may inspire future donation drives. People should be sure to thank everyone who donated. Running the drive is important work. But success relies on everyone who makes donations.

BENEFITS OF VOLUNTEERING

The most direct benefit of a donation drive is helping people experiencing homelessness. The organization receiving the items will get the items to the people who need them most. Those who donate and run the drive can feel good about helping their community.

There are other benefits too. Donation drives can become big events. They can draw a lot of attention. This can bring more awareness to homelessness. More people will become aware of the problem. They

Donation drives can help provide clothes to those in need.

may become interested in donating their

time or money in the future.

In 2020, three Pennsylvania teens set

up a donation drive. It was planned to

help women and children experiencing homelessness. They collected diapers, shampoo, children's books, and other items. They also accepted cash donations. They brought in more than $2,000 in all.

The teens set up donation bins at local schools. They also made a page on a fundraising website to take cash donations

MATCHING DONATIONS

Some companies will match their employees' donations to charity. People running donation drives can ask their donors to see if their companies do this. Matching donations can provide a big boost to a donation drive.

Donated clothes may be given to people impacted by natural disasters.

and further spread the word. On the page,

they wrote about what the donation drive

meant to them. They said, "We are so

grateful to have a chance to give back to a

community that has given us so much."[6]

MANY WAYS TO HELP

Homelessness remains a big problem in the United States. People in communities across the country do not have stable housing. But there are ways to help. People can volunteer at homeless shelters, giving others a warm, welcoming place to stay. They can help out at soup kitchens, making sure everyone has a hot meal to eat. They can participate in point-in-time counts, helping lawmakers understand the problem of homelessness in their communities. And they can run donation drives, collecting the supplies that people experiencing

Helping those experiencing homelessness is rewarding in many ways.

homelessness need most. All of these

things can help make a difference in the

lives of people experiencing homelessness.

GLOSSARY

background check
an investigation into someone's past

dignity
the state of being deserving of respect

economic
relating to the production and distribution of goods and services in a country

federal
having to do with the national government

hygiene
relating to keeping clean and healthy

misconceptions
misunderstandings or incorrect ideas about something

socialize
to spend time with someone and talk with him or her

substance use
the use of drugs

transitional
describing the period of change between two things

SOURCE NOTES

CHAPTER ONE: HOW CAN I VOLUNTEER AT A HOMELESS SHELTER?

1. Quoted in "OSH Volunteer Opportunities," *Our Saviour's Community Services*, 2021. https://oscs-mn.org.

2. Quoted in "Serving Families in Need at Center for the Homeless | Little Ways: Play," *Grotto*, n.d. https://grottonetwork.com.

CHAPTER TWO: HOW CAN I VOLUNTEER AT A SOUP KITCHEN?

3. Quoted Ann Paisley, "Interview with Michael Ottley, Director of Operations, Holy Apostles Soup Kitchen," *HuffPost*, April 6, 2017. www.huffpost.com.

4. "'A Humbling Experience.'—Nicholas," *Holy Apostles Soup Kitchen*, 2014. https://holyapostlessoupkitchen.org.

CHAPTER THREE: HOW CAN I VOLUNTEER WITH POINT-IN-TIME COUNTS?

5. Quoted in Patty Santos, "Pandemic Forces Cancellation of Point-in-Time Homeless Count in San Antonio," *KSAT*, January 11, 2021. www.ksat.com.

CHAPTER FOUR: HOW CAN I VOLUNTEER WITH A DONATION DRIVE?

6. "WCASD Home of the Sparrow Donation Drive," *GoFundMe*, 2020. www.gofundme.com.

FOR FURTHER RESEARCH

BOOKS

Cherese Cartlidge, *Homeless Youth*. San Diego, CA: ReferencePoint Press, 2017.

Emily Raij, *Kids Can Help Fight Poverty*. North Mankato, MN: Capstone Press, 2020.

INTERNET SOURCES

Melissa Carle, "Fighting Homelessness." *United Way*, December 2, 2019. www.unitedway.org.

"More Than a Number: Point-in-Time Counts Are Crucial Data," *SAMHSA*, June 16, 2020. www.samhsa.gov.

WEBSITES

Department of Health and Human Services (HHS): Homelessness
www.hhs.gov/programs/social-services/homelessness/index.html

The HHS website features links to research and resources about the problem of homelessness in the United States.

United States Interagency Council on Homelessness (USICH): Homelessness Statistics by State
www.usich.gov/tools-for-action/map

The USICH website includes statistics about homelessness in every US state.

RELATED ORGANIZATIONS

National Alliance to End Homelessness

1518 K St. NW, 2nd Floor
Washington, DC 20005
info@naeh.org
https://endhomelessness.org

The National Alliance to End Homelessness studies the problem of homelessness. It works with governments to figure out policy solutions. It also helps local communities develop programs that put those policies into practice. Its overall goal is to end homelessness in the United States.

National Coalition for the Homeless

2201 P St. NW
Washington, DC 20037
info@nationalhomeless.org
https://nationalhomeless.org

The National Coalition for the Homeless seeks to end homelessness while also making sure that people currently experiencing homelessness are cared for and protected. The organization educates the public and promotes policy changes. It also focuses on the areas of justice and civil rights for people experiencing homelessness.

INDEX

IMAGE CREDITS

ABOUT THE AUTHOR

Walt K. Moon is a writer who lives in Minnesota. He enjoys volunteering at his local library.